LENTEN COOKBOOK

QUICK & EASY VEGAN

40 RECIPES FOR 40 DAYS

by

Samar Wade

copyright Samar Wade

published 2020

Photos: mine

Contents

Breakfast	11
Lunch	13
Salads	15
Appetizers	20
Soup	22
Mediterranean	28
TexMex	37
Pasta	43
Fish	47
Dessert	49
Index	52

FORWARD

Have you ever wondered what kind of food you are going to make for Lent or even how you are going to get through it? I found myself asking this question quite often last year in 2019 being my first Eastern Orthodox Lent, and every time I would open the refrigerator, I would stare through it with a blank look of desperation in my face. I did for the most part cross the finish line vegan style (with the grace and mercy of God of course), but thought to myself that there must be an easier way to do this. In 2018, I returned from Roman Catholicism back to Eastern Orthodoxy and had to acquire different fasting habits. No meat, dairy, and eggs. No fish except for 2 days during Lent. No wine or olive oil on strict fast days. This essentially eliminated a lot of food that I regularly ate basically transforming my diet into a vegan one with the additional effort of skipping the wine and olive oil as well. So what in the world could I eat? Even more, what could my kids eat and what could I make for them? At this time during Lent 2020, and with the "stay-at-home" medical martial law order, it was time to put a plan into action. This plan helped me to get more organized, and by actually writing down the recipes I already knew and were familiar with in turn helped me to visualize the delectable treasures that were actually at my fingertips. This approach would result in less time wasted in coming up with a meal. Also, I didn't realize how many delicious recipes I already knew and had used in the past but for some reason fell out of use. Out of sight, out of mind, as we say. Many of these recipes were from my Mediterranean background which were learned from grandma including some personalized slight variations. Most recipes are very straight forward and easy to make. The only time consuming one would be the vegetarian grape leaves, but well worth it. Therefore, if the goal of Lent is to spend more time in fasting and prayer and less time in the kitchen, this book will help you do just that. Making these recipes for my family created enjoyable moments to sit together for meals, as my kids looked forward to each dinner. Remember the goal is to make meals easy, so if the recipe calls for making a dressing, you could decide to use an already made store bought dressing. If the task of making your own bread for sandwiches seems too daunting, you could buy a loaf of bread instead. The goal is to keep it simple. In some of the recipes, you could substitute frozen or canned vegetables for fresh. Try to adapt the recipes to best suit your needs. A grocery list is also included for the entirety of all the recipes in the book if you would like to buy everything ahead of time. It is divided into categories although it may not be feasible to get all the fresh fruits and vegetables at once.

This book is also written for vegans in mind, except for the two fish recipes of course. Vegans who are not fasting for Lent do not have to eliminate the olive oil and the wine.

About the oils, what kind of oils could be used for salads, cooking, stir frying, or baking? Giving up olive oil was something very difficult for me since nothing tastes quite the same. Being from the Mediterranean, we usually drown ourselves in olive oil because it is such an important staple to our diet and is used for almost everything. Also, I started researching healthy alternatives that could be used cold (for salads and toppings), and for cooking and baking. So I basically found 3 other healthy oils that could be substituted for olive oil which are flaxseed oil, avocado oil, and coconut oil. Flaxseed oil contains a lot of Omegas 3, 6, and 9 fatty acids and has a nuttiness that won't ruin the taste of salads and can be used for cold dishes. It is not a heat stable oil so it should not be used for cooking or baking. Coconut oil has a high smoke point up to 350 degrees and has antibacterial, antioxidant, and antiviral properties. It becomes solid under 70 degrees which can make it frustrating to work with, but has a very sweet taste that blends well with rice dishes, sautéing vegetables, and baking. Avocado oil has a high smoke point up to 520 degrees so it can be used for stir frying, sautéing, baking, and frying. It has a very mild taste so it blends well with food and doesn't stand out. It contains Vitamin E and Omega 9 fatty acid. Be careful of using grapeseed oil. Although it has an extremely high smoke point that is good for deep frying, you must make sure to get the kind that is naturally extracted (which costs more) verses the kind that is chemically extracted. The smoke point of any oil is the temperature where the oil starts burning and releases toxins and harmful free radicals in turn compromising the important benefits of the oil.

Remember to follow your Orthodox calendar because some fast days do allow wine and olive oil and for that reason olive oil is written in parentheses next to the fasting oil when it is allowed. Now you may ask, why all this attention to fasting detail? Isn't this just getting a bit nit-picky and going way overboard? In essence, fasting has more to do with the heart and paying attention with the mind rather than with the letter of the law so to speak. By checking our calendar, our mind begins to focus on what day it is, the saints and feasts of that day, so therefore in whatever we eat or abstain from, our hearts become released to be more attentive to God. Fasting encompasses our entire mind, heart, and body. May you have a Blessed Lent.

Shopping List

Oils

1 bottle olive oil

1 bottle avocado oil

1 bottle flaxseed oil

1 jar coconut oil

Spices

Salt

Sumac

Dry mint

Thyme

Italian seasoning

Rosemary

Garlic powder

Allspice

Cayenne pepper

Paprika

Black pepper

Curry powder

Cumin

Oregano

Bay leaves

Tarragon

Corriander

Chili powder

Red pepper flakes

Ginger

Perishable

¼ cup orange juice

24 medjool dates

1 bag pita bread

Non-perishable

1 box cream of wheat	1 box oatmeal
1 cup pecans	1 cup walnuts
1 jar honey	1 cup brown sugar
4 cups wheat flour	1 jar tahini
2 cups large burgol (cracked wheat)	2 cups orange lentils
3 tbs fine burgol (cracked wheat)	2 cups split peas
2 cups small dark brown lentils	7 cups brown rice
2 cups wide light brown lentils	2 boxes vegetable broth
1 jar grapeleaves	Squash seeds
1 bag tostada shells	1 package yeast
1 jar preserves	1 jar peanut butter
1 jar sunflower butter	2 jars spaghetti sauce
1 cup black olives	1 cup risotto
1 box veggie spaghetti	1 box vegetable rotini
1 box linguine	1 jar pesto
¼ cup sun dried tomatoes	¼ balsamic vinegar
½ c. apple cider vinegar	½ cup white wine
1 bottle lemon juice	2 tbs mustard

Non-perishable (cont'd)

2 jars salsa

1 bag corn chips

1 bag flour tortillas

Cans

8 cans chickpeas

2 cans fire-roasted diced tomatoes

1 can diced tomatoes with green chilies

1 can dark red kidney beans

1 can light red kidney beans

2 cans fat free refried beans

2 cans coconut milk

1 can canelli beans

8 cans diced tomatoes

1 can tri-blend beans

2 cans fava beans (foul)

5 cans black beans

1 can pinto beans

3 cans corn

Frozen

1 cup green beans

1 bag okra

3 bags mixed vegetables

2 cups cauliflower

1 bag peas

Fish

1 lb salmon

2 lbs cod

Vegetables

25 potatoes

4 sweet potatoes

36 onions

2 bunches green onion

41 garlics

25 tomatoes

1 cup grape tomatoes

3 green zucchini squash

2 yellow zucchini squash

1 spaghetti squash

4 green peppers

4 red peppers

3 yellow peppers

7 carrots

2 avocados

4 bunches parsley

1 bunch cilantro

1 bag arugula

1 bag romaine lettuce

5 bunches mint

4 cups spinach

1 cabbage

1 cup cauliflower

2 seedless cucumbers

5 lemons

3 limes

2 celery stalks

2 eggplants

Fruit

1 cup blueberries   1 cup raspberries

1 cup strawberries   1 apple

1 mango   1 banana

OUTSTANDING OATMEAL

½ cup oats

1 cup water

2 tbs pecans pieces

¼ cup blueberries

¼ cup raspberries

1 tbs honey

Put oatmeal and water in a bowl and microwave for 60 seconds. Remove from microwave, add the rest of the ingredients, and drizzle with honey.

Serves 1. Each serving has about 6 grams of protein and 41 mg of calcium.

FANTASTIC FARINA

1 cup water

1/3 cup farina (cream of wheat)

1 tbs brown sugar

¼ cup strawberries, quartered

1 tbs honey

Bring water, farina, and brown sugar to a boil stiring often as not to form lumps. Transfer to a bowl and top with strawberries and honey.

Serves 1. Each serving has about 7 grams of protein and 27 mg of calcium.

SCRUMPTUOUS SANDWICHES

Bread machine: 1 ½ cups water

2 tbs coconut oil   3 ¼ cups wheat flour

2 tbs brown sugar   1 tbs yeast

PB&J Sandwiches: *Sunflower Sandwiches:*

2 tbs peanut butter   2 tbs sunflower butter

2 tbs preserves   banana slices

apple slices   1 tbs honey

In bread machine, add wet ingredients first then the dry. Make a 1.5 pound loaf. When it's done slice into equal pieces. For PB&J sandwiches, spread peanut butter, then preserves, then top with apple slices. For the Sunflower sandwiches, spread sunflower butter, top with banana slices, and drizzle with honey.

Each PB&J serving has about 17 grams of protein and 57 mg of calcium.
Each Sunflower serving has about 17 grams of protein and 32 mg of calcium.

PIQUANT POTATO POTPOURRI

5 potatoes, peeled and chopped

1 green zucchini squash, sliced

1 tbs avocado oil (olive oil)

1 red bell pepper, sliced

1 yellow bell pepper, sliced

2 carrots, peeled and sliced

1 avocado, diced

2 cups water

1 onion, chopped

1 cup cauliflower

¼ tsp pepper

1 tsp sumac

½ tsp salt

Boil potatoes in water and cover until tender. In a large skillet, sauté onion in oil along with peppers, squash, carrots, and cauliflower until tender. Add potatoes with their juices and add spices and mix. Top with avocado.

Serves 5. Each serving has about 8 grams of protein and 59 mg of calcium.

TERRIFIC TABOULI

2 bunches flat leaf parsley, chopped

2 medium tomatoes, chopped

2 bunches green onion, chopped

1 small seedless cucumber, chopped

Small bunch fresh mint, chopped or 1 tbs dry mint

3 tbs fine cracked wheat

4 tbs flax oil (olive oil)

2 fresh lemons, squeezed or 4 tbs lemon juice

¼ tsp salt

Mix all ingredients. Let stand for about 25 minutes so the cracked wheat can soak up the juices. Mix again before serving.

Serves 4. Each serving has about 4 grams of protein and 126 mg of calcium.

FLAVORY FATOUSH

1 – 10 oz bag chopped romaine   3 tomatoes, chopped

1 cucumber, chopped   ½ onion, sliced

¼ cup parsley, chopped   1 tbs dry mint

3 tbs flax oil (olive oil)   4 tbs lemon juice

½ tsp salt   1 tbs sumac

1 pita bread

Add all ingredients and mix. Drizzle oil on pita and bake or fry. Break into pieces and mix into salad. Adjust to taste.

Serves 4. Each serving has about 4 grams of protein and 57 mg of calcium.

AMAZING ARUGULA

1 - 7 oz bag arugula   1 cup grape tomatoes, halved

1 cup corn, drained   ½ cup black olives

Dressing:

¼ cup flax oil (olive oil)   ¼ cup orange juice

¼ cup apple cider vinegar   2 tbs mustard

1 tbs honey   1 tsp thyme

¼ tsp salt   ¼ tsp black pepper   ½ tsp cumin

Put the first four ingredients in a large bowl. Put all ingredients of dressing in a jar and shake well. Pour on top of salad.

Serves 6. Each serving has about 2 grams of protein and 60 mg of calcium.

17

TANGY TOMATO SALAD

4 large tomatoes, chopped coarsely

1 onion, thinly sliced

1 cup fresh mint, chopped

2 tbs lemon juice

2 tbs flax oil (olive oil)

1 tsp sumac

½ tsp salt

Mix all ingredients thoroughly in a bowl. Adjust ingredients to taste. For a slight variation, add 1 chopped cucumber.

Serves 4. Each serving has about 1 gram of protein and 19 mg of calcium.

POSITIVELY POTATO SALAD

7 potatoes, peeled and chopped   3 cups water

½ cup parsley, chopped   ½ onion, chopped

¼ cup mint, chopped   3 garlic cloves, minced

3 tbs avocado oil (olive oil)   1 lemon, juiced

½ tsp salt   ¼ tsp black pepper

Boil potatoes in water until soft. Drain. Put in large bowl and add the rest of the ingredients while still hot and thoroughly mix. Adjust to taste.

Serves 4. Each serving has about 9 grams of protein and 84 mg of calcium.

BLISSFUL BABAGANOUSH

1 eggplant, baked

¼ tsp salt

1 garlic piece, minced

Juice of 1 small lemon

2 tbs tahini

Bake eggplant at 350 degrees for about an hour and 20 minutes or until soft. Remove from oven and cool about 20 minutes then peel. In bowl, mince garlic and salt together with a mortar. Then smash eggplant on top of garlic mixture. Mix with lemon juice and tahini. For a smoother texture, put in blender and pulse. Eat with pita bread. All ingredients are approximate and should be adjusted to taste.

Serves 2. Each serving has about 4 of grams of protein and 19 mg of calcium.

HEAVENLY HOMMOS

2 cans chickpeas

2 garlic pieces

2 tbs lemon juice or juice of 2 small lemons

4 tbs tahini

¼ tsp salt

Boil chickpeas along with juice from can until soft. When slightly cool, put in a food processor along with garlic, salt, and lemon juice and some of the chick pea juice. Blend. Add tahini. Adjust measurements to taste.

Serves 4. Each serving has about 6 grams of protein and 25 mg of calcium.

BRILLIANT BROWN LENTIL SOUP

1 tbs avocado oil (olive oil)

2 onions, chopped

2 cups brown lentils

½ cup brown rice

8 cups water

½ tsp salt

¼ tsp black pepper

In pot, sauté onions in oil until slightly brown sprinkling with half the salt and pepper. Rinse lentils and rice under cold water then add on top of onions with the rest of the ingredients. Bring to boil, cover with lid, turn on low heat, stirring often until all ingredients soften. Add more salt and pepper to taste.

Serves 8. Each serving has about 10 grams of protein and 28 mg of calcium.

SAVORY SPLIT PEA SOUP

2 tbs avocado oil (olive oil)

2 onions, chopped

2 cups, split peas

5 potatoes, peeled and chopped

10 cups water

½ tsp salt

¼ tsp black pepper

In a pot, boil the potatoes in 2 cups of water until tender. In another pot, sauté onions in oil until slightly brown. Add potatoes and the rest of the ingredients with 8 cups of water. Boil, then cover and simmer until tender, stirring occasionally.

Serves 5. Each serving has about 24 grams of protein and 74 mg of calcium.

LUMINOUS LENTIL SOUP

1 tbs avocado oil (olive oil)

2 cups orange lentils

10 cups water

½ tsp salt

2 onions, chopped

½ cup brown rice

2 carrots, chopped

¼ tsp pepper

Freshly squeezed lemon

In a large pot, sauté onions in oil until slightly brown. Add lentils, rice, salt, pepper, and 8 cups water. Bring it to a boil then cover and simmer. In a smaller pot, boil carrots in 2 cups of water until tender then add to soup mixture. Cook and stir until tender. Salt and pepper to taste. Add lemon juice in individual bowls if desired. Serve with crackers.

Serves 6. Each serving has about 18 grams of protein and 40 mg of calcium.

MOUTHWATERING MINESTRONE

1 tbs avocado oil (olive oil)

1 onion, chopped

4 garlic cloves, minced

1 zucchini, chopped

3 carrots, chopped

2 celery stalks, chopped

1 can diced tomatoes

2 tbs parsley, chopped

2 tsp oregano

1 tsp Italian seasoning

1 tsp thyme

1 tsp salt

½ tsp black pepper

6 cups vegetable broth

1 bay leaf

1 – 15 oz can canelli beans

1 cup frozen green beans

1 – 15 oz can red kidney beans

1 – 15 oz can chickpeas

1 cup spaghetti sauce

1 cup risotto

4 cups spinach, chopped

Sauté onion, garlic, zucchini, carrots, and celery until soft. Add the remaining ingredients except risotto and spinach. Stir, boil, then simmer. Add spinach and risotto and stir until risotto becomes al dente.

Serves 8. Each serving has about 12 grams of protein and 117 mg of calcium.

CULINARY CHILI

2 tbs avocado oil (olive oil)　　1 onion, chopped

½ green bell pepper, chopped　　2 garlic cloves, minced

¼ red bell pepper, chopped　　½ tsp oregano

1 – 15 oz can light red kidney beans　　1 tbs chili powder

1 – 15 oz can tri-bean blend　　1 tbs cumin

½ tsp cayenne pepper　　1 tbs paprika

¼ tsp black pepper　　1 tsp salt

¼ tsp red pepper flakes

2 – 14 oz cans fire-roasted diced tomatoes

Sauté onion, bell peppers, and garlic in oil until soft. Add tomatoes and beans. Add spices and stir until hot.

Serves 5. Each serving has about 12 grams of protein and 118 mg of calcium.

CHOICE CHICKPEA CURRY

1 tbs coconut oil

1 onion, chopped

3 cloves garlic, minced

2 – 15 oz cans chickpeas, drained

1 tbs ginger

1 tbs curry powder

1 – 14 oz can diced tomatoes

1 – 13 oz can coconut milk

2 cups frozen cauliflower

Sauté onion, garlic, and cauliflower in oil until light brown. Add chickpeas, spices, tomatoes, and stir. Add coconut milk. Stir until thoroughly heated. Salt to taste. Serve with millet or rice.

Serves 4. Each serving has 9 grams of protein and 73 mg of calcium.

BREATHTAKING BURGUL & TOMATO

1 onion, chopped

2 tbs avocado oil (olive oil)

1 can diced tomatoes or 2 large fresh tomatoes

2 cups large burgul (cracked wheat)

4 cups water

½ tsp salt

¼ tsp pepper

Sauté onion in oil until slightly brown then sauté tomatoes. Add the remainder of the ingredients, stir, then bring to a boil then cover. Set on low heat. Cook until burgol is tender.

Serves 4. Each serving has about 10 grams of protein and 37 mg of calcium.

MARVELOUS MNUZLEH

2 potatoes, peeled and chopped and boiled in 1 cup water

1 onion, quartered and sliced

2 tbs or more avocado oil (olive oil)

1 eggplant, peeled and sliced into ½ inch rounds

1 yellow zucchini squash, sliced into ½ inch rounds

1 – 15 oz can chickpeas

1 – 14 oz can diced tomatoes

½ tsp salt

Boil potatoes until tender. In a skillet, sauté onions in oil then add eggplant and sauté until tender. Add extra oil if eggplant sticks to pan. Add zucchini and sauté' slightly. Add the potatoes with their water and the remaining ingredients. Heat and thoroughly mix. Eat with pita bread.

Serves 4. Each serving has about 10 grams of protein and 69 mg of calcium.

MAGNIFICENT MJADERA

1 onion, chopped

4 tbs avocado oil (olive oil)

2 cups wide brown lentils

½ cup rice

7 cups water

½ tsp salt

¼ tsp pepper

1 onion, sliced

In a pot, sauté chopped onion in 2 tbs oil until light brown. Add lentils, rice, and water. Bring to boil, then simmer, cover, and stir frequently. When thickened, pour on plates. Sauté sliced onion with 2 tbs oil until brown and put on top of mjadera. Eat with pita bread.

Serves 6. Each serving has about 18 grams of protein and 50 mg of calcium.

30

FABULOUS FOUL

4 garlic cloves, minced

½ tsp salt

2 – 9 oz cans fava beans, not drained

1 – 15 oz can chickpeas, drained

3 tbs lemon juice

1 tbs flaxseed oil (olive oil)

1 tbs parsley, chopped

     Boil fava beans and chickpeas in a pot and stir. In a bowl, mince garlic with salt. Add bean mix to bowl. Partially smash and mix with lemon juice. Add more salt to taste. Top with oil and parsley. Eat with pita bread.

Serves 4. Each serving has about 12 grams of protein and 55 mg of calcium.

GORGEOUS GRAPE LEAVES

1 jar grape leaves or freshly picked

1 cup brown rice

1 – 15 oz can chickpeas, smashed

1 tsp salt

½ bunch flat parsley, chopped

2 tomatoes, chopped

1 cup avocado oil (olive oil)

½ cup lemon juice

1 onion, finely chopped

¼ tsp black pepper

¼ cup mint leaves, chopped

1 tsp allspice

Mix all the ingredients in a bowl except the grape leaves. Place a grape leaf with the veins up and put about a teaspoon of the mixture and roll it folding sides first. Arrange all grape leaves in a pot and pour leftover juices on top. Place a ceramic dish over them. Put enough water until it just covers the top of the grape leaves. Cover and cook on low heat about an hour until the inside of grape leaves are done. Remove plate adding extra oil or lemon juice for a tangy flavor.

Serves 4. Each serving has about 5 grams of protein and 55 mg of calcium.

LUCIOUS LOOBYA

2 tbs avocado oil (olive oil)

1 onion, sliced

3 garlic cloves, minced

2 tomatoes, chopped

1 lb frozen green beans

½ tsp salt

Sauté onion in oil until tender. Add garlic and tomatoes and sauté until tender. Add green beans and salt and cook until tender mixing frequently. Serve with pita bread or rice.

Serves 4. Each serving has about 2 grams of protein and 74 mg of calcium.

MELLOW MALFOOF

1 tbs avocado oil (olive oil)

1 onion, chopped

4 cups cabbage, chopped

½ tsp salt

2 cups brown rice

4 cups water

¼ tsp black pepper

1 tsp all-spice

Sauté onion in oil until slightly tender. Add cabbage and salt and sauté until tender. Add the rest of the ingredients. Stir then cover with lid until it boils then simmer until rice is done.

Serves 4. Each serving has about 7 grams of protein and 78 mg of calcium.

OUT-OF-THIS-WORLD OKRA

2 tbs avocado oil (olive oil)	2 onions, sliced
3 tomatoes, chopped	8 garlics, minced
1 cup spaghetti sauce	½ tsp salt
1 – 14 oz can vegetable broth	1 tsp coriander
1 - 16 oz bag frozen okra	1 tsp allspice

Sauté onions in oil until tender, then add tomatoes and sauté until soft. Add garlic and sauté. Add spaghetti sauce, broth, spices and stir. Add okra and cook until thoroughly heated. Serve with rice.

Serves 4. Each serving has about 5 grams of protein and 154 mg of calcium.

PRECIOUS PEAS

1 tbs avocado oil (olive oil)
3 garlics, chopped
1 cup water
1 – 16 oz bag frozen peas
½ tsp salt
1 tsp ground coriander

1 onion, sliced
3 tomatoes, chopped
3 potatoes, chopped
1 cup spaghetti sauce
¼ tsp black pepper

In a pot, boil potatoes in water until tender. Meanwhile, in a pan, sauté onion in oil on medium heat until slightly brown, then add garlic and sauté until tender. Add tomatoes to onion and sauté until soft. Add tender potatoes with its water. Add the rest of the ingredients. Stir and heat thoroughly. Serve with rice.

Serves 4. Each serving has about 10 grams of protein and 78 mg of calcium.

TASTY TOSTADAS

7 tostada shells

32 oz can fat free refried beans

16 oz jar salsa

1 large tomato, diced

2 cups lettuce, shredded

On each tostada spread ½ cup of refried beans. Then add 2 tablespoons of salsa on top of beans. Then add 2 tablespoons of diced tomato on top of salsa. Top with 2 tablespoons shredded lettuce.

* Optional – add chopped green onion and sliced black olives.

Serves 7. Each serving has about 10 grams of protein and 50 mg of calcium.

BOUNTIFUL BURRITOS

7 white flour tortillas about 8"

1 – 32 oz can fat free refried beans

2 cups cooked brown rice

1 green pepper, sliced

1 yellow pepper, sliced

1-2 tablespoons water

16 oz jar salsa

1 onion, sliced

1 red pepper, sliced

Stir refried beans with water to make smoother. Put ¼ cup of refried beans on a tortilla. Sprinkle ¼ cup rice on top. Add 1 tablespoon salsa and a few slices of onion, green, red, and, yellow peppers. Wrap it up and make 6 more.

*Optional – top with sliced olives and guacamole.

Serves 7. Each serving has about 11 grams of protein and 94 mg of calcium.

BEAUTIFUL BOTANA

1 – 13 oz bag white corn tortilla chips

1 – 15 oz can black beans, drained

1 – 15 oz can corn, drained

1 tomato, chopped

1 jar salsa

1 cup lettuce, chopped

3 olives

On a big plate, put a layer of chips, then 1/3 of the salsa, 1/3 of the black beans, 1/3 of the corn, and 1/3 of the tomato. Repeat 2 more times. Top with lettuce and olives.

Serves 4. Each serving has about 36 grams of protein and 465 mg of calcium.

COCONUT RICE WITH BLACK BEANS AND MANGO

2 onions, chopped			2 tbs avocado oil (olive oil)

2 cups brown rice			1 – 13 oz can coconut milk

1 1/2 cups water			1 tsp cumin

Black pepper to taste		Salt to taste

2 – 15 oz cans black beans, semi-drained

½ cup salsa				1 large tomato, chopped

1 mango				¼ cup cilantro, chopped

In a pot, sauté 1 chopped onion in 1 tbs oil. Add rice, coconut milk, water, salt, pepper, and ½ tsp cumin. Bring to boil, cover, and turn on low heat until rice is done. In another pot, sauté the other onion in 1 tbs oil. Add black beans, salt, pepper, and 1 tbs cumin and stir. Cover and set on low heat. When rice is finished, put in a casserole dish, top with black bean mix, salsa, tomato, mango, and cilantro.

Serves 6. Each serving has about 7 grams of protein and 60 mg of calcium.

STUPENDOUS SOUTHWEST MIX

1 tbs avocado oil (olive oil)   1 onion, chopped

1 green pepper, chopped   ½ red pepper chopped

½ yellow pepper, chopped   ½ tsp salt

1 – 15 oz can corn   1 – 15 oz can pinto beans

¼ tsp red pepper flakes   ¼ tsp black pepper

1 – 10 oz can diced tomatoes with green chilies

Sauté onion and peppers with salt in oil until soft. Add the rest of the ingredients and stir until thoroughly heated. Serve with chips or tortillas.

Serves 4. Each serving has about 9 grams of protein and 71 mg of calcium.

SUPERBLY STUFFED SWEET POTATO

4 sweet potatoes, baked	1 onion, chopped
1 tbs avocado oil (olive oil)	1 tomato, chopped
2 - 15 oz cans black beans	½ tsp salt
¼ tsp black pepper	1 tbs cumin
½ cup cilantro, chopped	1 avocado, chopped
3 limes, squeezed	4 tsp salsa

Bake potatoes on 350 degrees for about 70 minutes or until tender. While potatoes are baking, sauté onion in oil until tender then add tomatoes and sauté until slightly tender. Add beans, salt, and cumin. Heat thoroughly and stir frequently. Take off heat and add cilantro, avocado, and juice of 2 limes. Stir. Cut baked potatoes in half squeezing extra lime juice on top. Add ¼ of the mixture over each potato. Top each with 1 tsp of salsa.

Serves 4. Each serving has about 43 grams of protein and 400 mg of calcium.

PALATABLE PESTO SPAGHETTI

1 -12 oz box of veggie spaghetti, cooked al dente

2 tbs avocado oil (olive oil)

1 onion, chopped

1 garlic, minced

1 - 12 oz package mixed frozen vegetables

1 – 6 oz jar pesto

1 tbs Italian seasoning

     While pasta is cooking, sauté onion in a skillet with oil until light brown, then sauté garlic with it. Add vegetables and mix until tender. Drain the spaghetti and mix with pesto. Add the vegetables and mix. Sprinkle with Italian seasoning.

Serves 6. Each serving has about 14 grams of protein and 109 mg of calcium.

RAVISHING ROTINI

1 – 12 oz box vegetable rotini	½ red bell pepper, chopped

½ green bell pepper, chopped	1 tomato, chopped

¼ cup black olives, pitted	1/8 cup sun dried tomatoes

Dressing:

2 tsp Italian seasoning	*1 garlic clove, minced*

¼ cup balsamic vinegar	*¼ cup apple cider vinegar*

1 tsp parsley	*½ cup flax oil*

1 tsp minced onion	*1 tsp garlic powder*

1 tsp mustard	*1 tsp honey*

Cook pasta according to package directions and drain. Put the dressing ingredients in a jar and shake. In a big bowl, combine warm pasta with all ingredients. Mix well. For shortcut, use store bought Italian dressing instead.

Serves 6. Each serving has about grams of 12 protein and 34 mg of calcium.

LOVELY LINGUINE

1 – 1 lb package linguine

1 tbs avocado oil (olive oil)

2 garlic cloves, chopped

2 – 15 oz cans diced tomatoes

1 tsp tarragon

2 onions, sliced

½ tsp salt

1 tsp oregano

1 tsp basil

1 tbs Italian seasoning

Cook linguine according to package directions. Meanwhile in a skillet, sauté onions and oregano in oil until soft. Add garlic and basil and sauté until brown. Add tomatoes, salt, and tarragon, and stir until hot. Drain linguine and put in a big bowl. Mix in Italian seasoning, then add the tomato mixture and mix.

Serves 4. Each serving has about 17 grams of protein and 29 mg of calcium.

SPECTACULAR SPAGHETTI SQUASH

1 spaghetti squash 1 tbs avocado oil

1 onion, chopped 2 garlic cloves, chopped

1 tomato, diced 1 – 15 oz can chick peas

1 – 24 oz jar spaghetti sauce 2 tsp basil

2 tsp Italian spices 2 tsp rosemary

1 tsp garlic powder

    Bake spaghetti squash at 350 degrees for about an hour or until tender. Meanwhile, in skillet sauté onion and garlic in oil until tender then add tomato and sauté until slightly tender. Add chickpeas, spaghetti sauce, and half of the spices, except garlic powder. Stir and keep warm. After squash is tender, remove from oven, split in half, and put seeds in bowl to use for another recipe. In a casserole dish, scrape out squash using a fork. Mix with the other half of the spices including garlic powder. Spread sauce mixture on top of squash and sprinkle with rosemary.

Serves 4. Each serving has about 9 grams of protein and 102 mg of calcium.

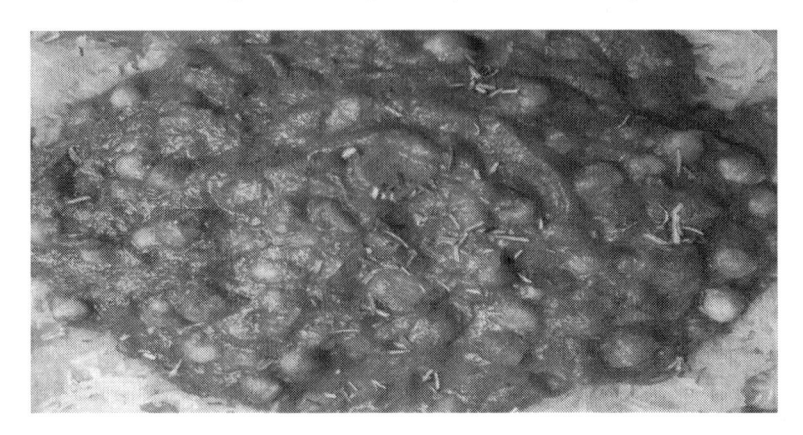

FESTIVE FEAST OF THE ASSUMPTION FISH

2 lbs cod or any fish

3 bags mixed frozen vegetables

3 tbs olive oil

Salt

Pepper

Red pepper flakes

Grease the bottom of a large 9x13 casserole dish. Salt and pepper the fish to taste and place in dish. On top, place the frozen vegetables. Drizzle oil on top. Add spices to taste. Place uncovered in oven at 350 degrees about 50 minutes or until fish is tender.

Serves 6. Each serving has about 29 grams of protein and 58 mg of calcium.

TANTALIZING TOMATO & ONION FISH

1 lb salmon or any fish	**½ cup white wine**
2 tbs olive oil	**2 tsp Italian seasoning**
2 tsp tarragon	**1 tsp garlic powder**
1 tsp salt	**½ tsp black pepper**
½ tsp red pepper flakes	**1 onion, sliced**
1 yellow zucchini, sliced	**1 tomato, chopped**
1 green zucchini, sliced	**2 garlic cloves, minced**

Put fish in an oiled casserole dish and top with half the wine, oil, and spices. Start bake at 350 degrees for about 30 minutes. While fish is baking, sauté onion, tomato, zucchinis, and garlic in the other half of the oil in a skillet until soft. Add the other half of the wine and spices and stir. Put mixture on top of fish and bake for another 15 minutes or until tender.

Serves 4. Each serving has about 33 grams of protein and 82 mg of calcium.

SENSATIONAL SQUASH SEEDS

Spaghetti squash seeds

½ tsp avocado oil

Salt to taste

Hallow out the seeds from the inside of a cooked spaghetti squash. You could save them from the Spectacular Spaghetti Squash Recipe. Clean them off and dry them on a paper towel for 24 hours. Put them in a small bowl with oil and salt and mix. Spread them on a baking tray and toast them until light brown.

Serves 2. Each serving has about 3 grams of protein and 20 mg of calcium.

DELIGHTFUL DATES

24 medjool dates, pitted

1 cup walnuts or pecans

Remove pits from all the dates. Stuff dates with nuts and close. Arrange on plate.

Serves 7. Each date has about 2 grams of protein and 18 mg of calcium.

Index

Arugula, 17

Babaganoush, 20

Black Beans & Mango, 40

Botana, 39

Burgol & Tomato, 28

Burritos, 38

Chickpeas, 21, 27

Cabbage, 34

Chickpea Curry, 27

Chili, 26

Cream of Wheat, 11

Dates, 50

Eggplant, 20, 29

Farina, 12

Fatoush, 16

Fava Beans, 31

Fish, 47, 48

Grape Leaves, 32

Green Beans, 33

Hommos, 21

Lentil, 22, 23, 24, 30

Linguine, 45

Minestrone, 25

Mjaderah, 30

Mnuzleh, 29

Oatmeal, 11

Okra, 35

Pasta

    Linguine, 45

    Pasta Salad, 44

    Pesto Spaghetti, 43

Pasta Salad, 44

Peanut butter, 13

Peas, 36

Pesto Spaghetti, 43

Potatoes, 7

Potato Salad, 19

Rotini, 44

Sandwiches, 13

Soups

    Brown Lentil, 22

    Chili, 26

    Green Lentil, 23

    Minestrone, 25

    Orange Lentil, 24

    Split Pea, 23

Southwest Mix, 41

Spaghetti, 43

Spaghetti Squash, 46

Split Pea Soup, 23

Squash Seeds, 49

Sunflower butter, 13

Sweet Potato, 42

Tabouli, 15

Tomato Salad, 18

Tostadas, 38

Printed in Great Britain
by Amazon